CREATING THE WEDDING OF YOUR DREAMS

JUDI WILLIAMS

CONTENTS

BRIDAL SHOWER AND LUNCHEON
PAGE 4

This chapter presents table centerpieces and floral arrangements for your bridal shower, as well as instructions for making pretty party favors and napkin rings. There are even recipes for a delightful luncheon for eight.

WEDDING CEREMONY
PAGE 24

Whether it is to be an elegant candlelight service or a garden wedding indoors, you will find ideas here for both. There are also ways to add a special touch to your wedding ceremony.

RECEPTION

PAGE 36

*Make your wedding reception
memorable with these ideas for decor,
flowers, table settings and party favors.
There is even a wedding flag to guide
your guests to the reception venue.*

MEMORIES

PAGE 52

*Preserve the beauty of your wedding
day with these delightful mementos made
from the wedding flowers. There are even
decorator items for your new home – all
made with souvenirs of your special day.*

Shower and Luncheon

Who an exciting time in your life!
You have found that special person
you want to spend your life with and
now you are making plans for the
wedding of your dreams!
Bridal showers and luncheons are
a great opportunity for friends
and family to get together
before the wedding.
This chapter will give you many
unique ideas for a formal or garden
shower, ways to decorate a setting for
a bridal luncheon in honor of your
bridesmaids and a tea plate luncheon
with recipes included!
Delight in this special time when
friends and loved ones gather to
celebrate with you.

JUDI

ELEGANT BRIDAL SHOWER

If you are planning an elegant, formal wedding for your big celebration day, you will also want to carry through that theme for your shower. This table (pictured pages 4-5) is stunning and is very easy to achieve with a few yards of fabric and beautiful ribbon. Add a luxurious bouquet of flowers and soft candlelight, and the mood is set! The gold lamé, net and wired ribbon can be used over and over again.

MATERIALS

large white tablecloth
1 large and 1 small sturdy box
4-6 yards gold lamé fabric
6-8 yards white net
4-6 yards white and gold wired ribbon
4-5 yards gold braid
floral arrangement (details below)
cherub (optional)

INSTRUCTIONS

1 This table is layered for impact. Place the white cloth on the table with the large sturdy box underneath, near the back, on the left side. This will be the platform for the flowers. Place the smaller box in front of the large one if you are using a cherub.

2 Arrange the gold lamé over the white cloth. Don't smooth it out, but allow it to drape and billow, creating a graceful flow. If you tuck the raw edges under, you won't need a hem.

3 Arrange the white net over the gold lamé in big puffs to add the soft romantic look to the table.

4 Twist and curl the white and gold wired ribbon and the gold braid through the puffs of net. The wired ribbon is terrific to work with, holding any shape you mold it to.

DRAMATIC FLORAL CENTERPIECE

MATERIALS

large vase
10 stems tree fern
12 stems long, slender larkspur
6 stems white stock
12 stems Queen Anne's lace
6 stems of white, miniature carnations
12 stems white scabiosa (medium-sized flower)
12 long-stemmed white roses
sturdy box
tablecloth
white net
wired ribbon
gold braid
pair of tall candlesticks
pair of white candles
cherub (optional)

INSTRUCTIONS

1 Fill the vase with water and add a floral preservative. Cut each flower stem individually, on a slant, and place it immediately in the water. Cut each stem at different heights to give a high-low effect. Start forming your arrangement with the tree fern, tall larkspur and stock.

2 Fill in with Queen Anne's lace, miniature carnations, adding scabiosa flowers and roses last.

3 To achieve the raised look, place the sturdy box under the tablecloth and set the floral arrangement on top to make an even more dramatic effect. Arrange the white net in big puffs around the base of the vase.

4 Tie a 36" length of wired ribbon and gold braid around the neck of the vase. Twist and curl the ends down the side of the arrangement and onto the table.

5 Position a pair of tall candlesticks with candles on either side.

GARDEN TABLE

If you are planning the beautiful garden wedding that you have always dreamed about, follow the garden theme through for your shower as well. A friend of mine, Marsha Allen, created this wonderful garden fence centerpiece to give an English garden look to your table. It is very easy and your guests will be delighted!

MATERIALS

section of wooden border fencing (our fence is 12" x 36")
similar length of styrofoam
1 bunch of large green leaves
1 bunch of tall bear grass
moss
2 tall, slender silk flowers
2 medium-length, slender silk flowers
6 silk roses
6 bunches of silk violets
6 filler flowers such as daisies or lilies
2 bunches of silk ivy
bird and nest
glue gun

INSTRUCTIONS

1 Place the wooden fence on top of the styrofoam and push it in as far as possible. Glue it firmly into place.

2 Glue on the moss to completely cover the styrofoam.

3 Glue the ivy and other greens to the styrofoam base on both sides of the fence. Make sure they are at various heights.

4 Push the silk flowers into the styrofoam base on both sides of the fence. Arrange them for a high-low effect, as they would grow in a garden.

5 Tuck the bird and nest into the greens and glue them in place.

Another special touch is a ribbon garland of leaves. Collect some shiny green leaves and staple them to a long ribbon. Overlap them slightly to conceal the staples. Drape the garland along the table, tucking in a few fresh flowers to complete the picture.

Party Favors with Ribbon Roses

For that final touch to your garden bridal shower, add one of these beautiful party favors, designed by Sharon Ruth of Rolf Gille Imports in San Francisco, California. Adorned with ribbon roses and filled with candy or nuts, they will be a great memento of your special day.

Party Favor

MATERIALS

For each favor

9" diameter scalloped circle of iridescent tulle

two 9" diameter tulle circles in a color of your choice

clothespin

1 yard instant bow ribbon

tiny (1$\frac{1}{2}$" across) plastic dish for candy or nuts

3 sugar-coated candy or nuts

1 ribbon rose and leaf

INSTRUCTIONS

1 Place the scalloped tulle circle on a flat surface. Place one colored tulle circle on top. Put the tiny plastic dish off-center, about 3" from the bottom edge of the tulle. Place the candy or nuts in the dish.

2 Gather the tulle over the candy, holding it together with a clothespin. Knot one end of the instant bow ribbon firmly around the tulle, just above the candy. Remove the clothespin. The tulle will be slightly lower at the front.

3 Place the remaining colored tulle circle on a flat surface and gather it, accordion-style, across the center. Tie the gathered center at an angle to the front of the favor. Tie on a ribbon rose.

4 Push the ribbon along the gathering cord on the instant bow ribbon to make a dazzling bow. Tie the cord around the tulle to hold it in place and trim the cord ends close to the favor.

5 Fluff up the tulle by pulling the tulle layers apart.

Gathered Purple Rose

MATERIALS

For each rose

12" length of 1" wide wired ribbon

pearl stamen

florists' tape

glue gun

INSTRUCTIONS

1 Carefully pull the wire from one edge of the 12" length of wired ribbon. Push the ribbon along the wire towards the center from both ends at the same time, until the ribbon is 8" long.

2 Tie the wires together in a knot and glue the raw ends of the ribbon together to form a circle. Fold this circle in half to give a double thickness of ribbon.

3 Place the pearl stamen on the gathered edge and glue it in place.

4 Wrap the two thicknesses of ribbon around the pearl stamen and glue securely in place. Wrap the ribbon and stamen wires together with florists' tape.

FOLDED PINK ROSE

MATERIALS

For each rose

15" length of 1" wide wired ribbon
1 pearl stamen
florists' tape
glue gun

INSTRUCTIONS

1 Take the 15" length of wired ribbon and fold one end down diagonally to conceal the raw edge. Place the pearl stamen over the fold, with the top of the pearls even with the top of the ribbon. Wrap the end of the ribbon tightly around the stamen to form the center of the rose. (See Illustration 1, pages 68-69.)

2 Place your right thumb under the ribbon, close to the stamen. (See Illustration 2, pages 68-69.)

3 Rotate the ribbon-wrapped stamen counter-clockwise towards your thumb. Let the ribbon slide along your thumb until the ribbon automatically forms a diagonal fold. (See Illustration 3, pages 68-69.)

4 Keep your thumb and index finger in the position shown in Illustration 3. Pressing your index finger down, rotate your hand away from you a half-turn. The ribbon will slide and curl over your thumb. At the same time, rotate the stamen counter-clockwise with your left hand. Repeat this procedure over and over until 1" of ribbon is left. Secure this end under the rose by wrapping the wire around the base of the stamen. Wrap it with florists' tape for a neat finish.

Don't be discouraged if your first rose doesn't look great, just take it apart and practice until you are happy with the result.

SHIRRED PEACH ROSE

MATERIALS

For each rose

12" length of 1" wide wired ribbon
1 pearl stamen
florists' tape
glue gun

INSTRUCTIONS

1 Take the 12" length of wired ribbon and carefully pull the wire from one edge of the ribbon. Push the ribbon along the wire towards the center from both ends at the same time, until the ribbon is 8" long.

2 With the shirred side down, fold one end of the shirred ribbon to the inside to conceal the raw edge. Place the pearl stamen on top of the fold. (See Illustration 1, pages 68-69.)

3 Wrap the ribbon around the stamen to create a tight center. Continue to wrap it, loosening the ribbon as you go around, to achieve an open look to your rose. (See Illustration 2, pages 68-69.)

4 Knot the wires together and glue them to hold the flower in place. Wrap the ribbon and stamen wires together with florists' tape.

FRENCH RIBBON LEAVES

MATERIALS

For each leaf

5" length of 1" wide wired ribbon
florists' wire
heavy gauge wire for the stem
glue gun
florists' tape

INSTRUCTIONS

1 Carefully pull the wire from one edge of the ribbon. Push the ribbon along the wire towards the center from both ends at the same time, until the ribbon is $2^1/2$" long.

2 Knot the wires together and glue the gathered edges together on the back.

3 Pinch the ribbon together at the base of the leaf and wrap it with florists' wire to hold it in place. Wrap it again with a heavier wire to form a stem. Cover the stem with florists' tape.

BRIDAL LUNCHEON

Your bridal luncheon can be wonderfully feminine and unique to you. This lovely setting is a treat for your sense of smell, as well as a feast for your eyes and is a wonderful way to display any collection you have, such as colored glass or porcelain figurines.

Notice the use of the pedestal plate to add the important high-low effect to the arrangement.

MATERIALS

colored tablecloth
lace cloth
small pedestal plate
small teapot
fresh garden flowers
cherub or other appropriate figurine
4 cups and saucers (all different floral patterns)

INSTRUCTIONS

1 Set your table with a lovely, colored tablecloth. Place the lace cloth over the top. Position the small pedestal plate in the center to lift up the teapot and add height to your arrangement.

2 Place the teapot and lid on the plate and fill it with water and flowers. Place some flowers around the edge of the plate and add a cherub or some other little figurine.

3 Arrange the cups and saucers around the base of the pedestal plate. Fill them with water and flowers.

Be ready for the compliments!

14

TABLE TREATS

PARTY FAVORS

Create a festive atmosphere with this beautiful party favor and napkin ring, designed by Sharon Ruth of Rolf Gille Imports of San Francisco, California. They are so easy to make and are a wonderful way to thank your guests for sharing this special day with you. This setting features another lovely touch – flowers and lace pressed under the glass for a special luncheon plate.

MATERIALS

For each favor
24" shirring ribbon
24" of 1^1/2" wide wired ribbon
1 pearl stamen
sugar-coated almonds or other candy
10" tube ribbon

INSTRUCTIONS

1 Make a shirred ribbon rose by carefully pulling the string from both ends of the ribbon at the same time until the ribbon is completely gathered. Wrap the ribbon around the pearl stamen, following the instructions for the shirred ribbon rose on pages 68-69.

2 Tie a bow from the wired ribbon following the instructions on pages 70-71.

3 Place the almonds or other candy in the tube ribbon and fold it into thirds. Place the shirred ribbon rose in the center of the bow and attach them both to the candy-filled tube with the wire from the pearl stamen.

NAPKIN RINGS

MATERIALS

For each napkin ring
30" of 1^1/2" wide wired ribbon
1^3/4" dowel or cardboard paper towel tube
clothespin
24" shirring ribbon

INSTRUCTIONS

1 Wrap the wired ribbon around a length of dowel or cardboard paper towel tube. Fasten with a clothespin.

2 Gather the shirring ribbon by pulling the string from both ends at the same time. Tie the string ends to the wired ribbon between the clothespin and the dowel or tube.

3 Tie the ends of the wired ribbon in a bow. Cut the ribbon tails in a V shape. Remove the dowel or tube and place a napkin in the loop.

DECORATIVE LUNCHEON PLATE

The glass plates are fun and easy to do! Place a lace doily (either cloth or paper) in the center of a glass plate. Arrange a few fresh or silk flowers and leaves on top of the doily. You can also twist some ribbon through the flowers if you like. Place another glass plate on top. The top plate should be clear in the center so you can see the flowers.

Try this at Christmas with some holly and red ribbon!

TEA PLATE LUNCHEON

Now that you have decorated your table, make sure the food for your special luncheon is perfect! We found a delightful little tea room that serves a delicious "tea plate". The Country Court Tea Room in Capitola, California, is one of those wonderful places that you return to again and again.

The friendly proprietress, Donna DesJarlais, shares with us some of her special recipes, handed down from her family in Nashville, Tennessee. Each of these recipes serves eight guests.

SPINACH SOUP

INGREDIENTS

3 tablespoons butter
6 tablespoons chopped onion
2 packages frozen chopped spinach
3 cups chicken broth
2 cups milk
sherry
salt and white pepper

METHOD

1 Place the butter, onions, spinach and chicken broth in a saucepan and cook until the spinach is completely thawed. Do not overcook. Purée.

2 Add milk, sherry and salt and pepper to taste. May be served hot or cold.

CHICKEN SALAD SANDWICH

INGREDIENTS

1 1/4 cups slivered almonds, roasted
2 1/2 cups chopped chicken (roast chicken gives the best flavor)
2 1/2 cups finely chopped celery
1 cup mayonnaise
freshly ground black pepper
whole wheat or white bread, thinly sliced

METHOD

1 Roast the almonds on a cookie sheet at 350°F for 15 minutes.

2 Trim the crusts from the bread. Mix the filling and spread on the bread. Cut the sandwich in half and cover with a damp towel, if not serving immediately. Put one half of a sandwich on each tea plate.

TOMATO ROUNDS

INGREDIENTS

3 or 4 small ripe tomatoes, sliced
loaf of thinly sliced white bread
onion mayonnaise (1 cup mayonnaise with 1/4 cup finely chopped onions)
freshly ground black pepper

METHOD

Trim the crusts from the bread and using a biscuit cutter, cut quantity of bread into rounds. Spread each round with the onion mayonnaise and top with tomato slice. Season with black pepper to taste. These sandwiches must be made just before serving.

FROZEN FRUIT SALAD

INGREDIENTS

1 pint sour cream
2 tablespoons lemon juice
1/2 cup sugar
1 medium banana, chopped
9 oz can of crushed pineapple, including juice
1/4 cup maraschino cherries, chopped, juice reserved
4 strawberries, halved

METHOD

1 Place sour cream, lemon juice, sugar, banana, pineapple and cherries in a bowl and mix to combine. Add cherry juice until you achieve the shade of pink you want.

2 Place fruit salad mixture in cupcake papers in muffin tins and freeze. Remove cupcake papers. Place the frozen fruit salad on a bed of lettuce and top with half a strawberry.

POTATO CHIP COOKIES

INGREDIENTS

1 lb butter
1 cup sugar
3¹/2 cups flour
2 teaspoons vanilla essence
2 cups potato chips, crushed
powdered sugar

METHOD

1 Place the butter and sugar in a bowl and beat until creamy, then gradually add the flour and vanilla.

2 Mix in the potato chips, then form the mixture into small balls.

3 Place the balls 1" apart on a lightly-greased cookie sheet and press down using the back of a teaspoon. Bake at 325°F for about 12 minutes. Allow them to cool, then sift powdered sugar on each cookie.

CELEBRATE WITH YOUR BRIDESMAIDS

The idea for this gorgeous centerpiece, featuring a collection of perfume bottles, came from our photographer, Todd Tsukushi. We asked him to recreate the look for you.

CENTERPIECE

MATERIALS

small pedestal plate
lace tablecloth
collection of perfume bottles of various shapes and sizes
1¹/₂ yards gold braid
small amount of potpourri
votive candles in glass containers

INSTRUCTIONS

1 Set the pedestal plate in the center of the lace tablecloth covered table. Arrange the perfume bottles on top of the plate and around the base.

2 Twist the gold braid through the arrangement of bottles and down onto the table.

3 Sprinkle fragrant potpourri around the perfume bottles and on the lace cloth. Place the votive candles around for a romantic effect. If you have extra gold braid, tie a short piece around the napkins with a square knot and fringe the ends.

GIFT WRAPS

MATERIALS

boxes of appropriate sizes
sufficient fabric (the amount will vary with the size of the box); we used lavender moiré taffeta, pink satin and burgundy velvet
wired ribbon in colors to match
pearl stamens
silk rose and greens
craft glue or spray-on glue
glue gun

INSTRUCTIONS

1 Wrap the lid and bottom of the boxes separately so the box can be used again and again. Glue the fabric to the box for best results.

2 Decorate each box with color-coordinated wired ribbon. The pink box has a ribbon rose tucked into the bow. It was made from a 12" length of wired ribbon. Carefully pull the wire from one edge of the ribbon. Push the ribbon along the wire towards the center from both ends at the same time. Tie the ends to secure. Glue the raw edges of the ribbon together. Begin by folding one end over to conceal the raw edge. Place a pearl stamen on top of the fold and tightly roll the end two turns to form the center of the rose. Gently gather the rest of the ribbon in your fingers around this center, gradually turning as you go. Hold the rose together by twisting with the wire and then gluing. Glue this rose and silk greens on to the bow.

The lavender box has two rosebuds made of fabric. Cut two lengths of fabric, each 4" x 12" long. Fold each one in half to give you two

strips, each 2" x 12". Tightly roll one end of one strip for two turns around a pearl stamen to form the center of the flower. Gather the rest of the strip in your fingers around this center, turning the stamen gradually as you go. Glue the strip in several spots to hold the rosebud together. Make the other one the same. Glue the rosebuds to the top of the box, around the bow. Add silk greens if you like.

For the burgundy velvet package, glue a lovely silk rose into the gold bow for a stunning effect. See pages 70-71 for instructions to make the bow.

CHANDELIER BOW

Decorate your chandelier or light to create a festive mood, or embellish a vase of flowers with a bow to give extra flair to your shower table.

MATERIALS

10 yards 1 1/2" wide florists' ribbon
florists' wire

INSTRUCTIONS

1 Make two large basic bows with five loops on each side, following the instructions on page 70. Leave the tail 30" long. Secure the bow with wire.

2 Tie each bow to a 2-yard length of ribbon. Wire the bows back-to-back on either side of the chandelier chain, right up against the ceiling. Add extra streamers by passing the ribbon through the chandelier chain under the bow. Cut the ends on the diagonal.

FLOWER BOW

MATERIALS

6 yards 1 1/2" wide florists' ribbon
florists' wire

INSTRUCTIONS

1 Make a basic bow with five loops on each side, following the instructions on pages 70-71. Cut the tail on the bow to 30". Secure with wire, leaving the ends long.

2 Tie the bow with a 2-yard length of ribbon. Tuck the wire ends inside the vase of flowers to hold the bow in place. Cascade the ribbon ends down the vase and onto the table. Cut the ends on the diagonal.

INVITATIONS

Verify the date and time with the church and reception location before you place the order for the invitations. It is a good idea to order an extra twenty invitations. Ask the printer to deliver the envelopes as soon as possible so you can begin addressing them even before the invitations arrive. Addresses should be handwritten in black ink. If you would like a single person to bring a guest, add "and guest". Include a map of the location of the ceremony and reception for out-of-town guests.

The Wedding Ceremony

A wedding is a wonderful celebration of two separate lives becoming one, creating a new home and family. Taking on many of the tasks and being involved yourself is one way of ensuring your wedding reflects your personality. This chapter is designed to stimulate your imagination and give you some ideas. There are also pretty bridal accessories that are fun and easy for you to make yourself. All your planning will ensure that you enjoy every moment of your special wedding day.

JUDI

ELEGANT CANDLELIGHT WEDDING

My daughter, Julie, and her fiancé, Byron McGaha, wanted an elegant candlelight wedding. The romantic mood was set with tall, ivory-colored taper candles nestled among the beautiful flowers and ivy across the front of the sanctuary. Large brass candelabras adorned each side, and tall silk trees, glistening with tiny white lights, stood behind the flowers.

MATERIALS

extra long table, about 8'
boxes and blocks for supporting the arrangement
tablecloth (optional)
plastic sheeting
white net (optional)
13 dark-colored plastic containers with oasis for the fresh flowers
100 large flowers with long stems (we used white spider mums)
4 large bunches of baby's breath
7 bunches of tree fern
12 tall taper candles for the table plus candles for the candelabras and centre aisle
12 tall hurricane glasses to go around candles
lots of English ivy and long slender ferns
tall silk trees
tiny white lights

INSTRUCTIONS

1 Put the long table in place. Drape it with a cloth if the table legs are not attractive. You might want to layer the table cover with yards and yards of white net billowing down onto the floor. Be sure to protect the table top with plastic.

2 Soak each oasis in water and place in each plastic container, adding extra water. Cut the flower stems one at a time and place the flowers immediately into each oasis. Leave the stems longer in the center of the arrangement and taper them slightly on the sides and front of the arrangement. There is no need to place flowers at the back of the arrangement as they will not be seen. Fill in around the flowers with the delicate baby's breath and

tree fern, reserving some of these for later.

3 The key to this table arrangement is to achieve different levels by using small boxes and wooden blocks of various sizes. The center container at the back of the table should be the highest point. The flowers on the left and right back corners should be slightly lower, halfway between the center and the front corners of the table. Place the other containers in a pleasing manner to fill in.

4 Place the candles with hurricane glasses in among the flowers, lifting some up on boxes at different levels to achieve a high-low effect.

5 Tuck in some long stems of ivy and fern, allowing them to cascade over the edge of the table. Be sure the plastic containers are hidden by the greens. Tuck in more baby's breath and tree fern among the flowers to give a soft, wispy look.

6 Place tall silk trees in the background and load them with tiny white lights. These lights look best if they are placed along the branches with an "in-and-out" positioning rather than pulled tight in a straight line. Be sure to plug them in as you arrange them so you can see how they look.

"Keep love in your heart. A life without it is like a sunless garden when the flowers are dead."

Oscar Wilde

A Garden Wedding Indoors

Have you always dreamed of having a garden wedding but were afraid to trust the weather outdoors? Or have you dreamed of being married in your church, yet wanted a garden setting? Veronica and Devin Eckhardt solved this dilemma and created a beautiful garden setting indoors for their wedding.

Choose a variety of items with an outdoors feel, such as a gazebo, an arch, white picket fences, garden bench and garden statues. What you choose will be determined, to some extent, by the space you have to work with.

Buy plants from the nursery and leave them in their containers. Place some 4" pots of petunias and pansies in front of the larger plants to hide the plastic containers. Feature a few special terracotta planters but do not remove the plants from their plastic containers. Choose as many different shapes and sizes of plants as you can in the colors to complement your color scheme. Be sure to have some dark colors, such as purple and blue, to add depth to the garden look. Mix in green silk trees, if you wish.

Place the plants in clusters, just as they would grow in a natural garden setting. Set some of them up on boxes to add height and to give a high-low effect. In the wedding shown here, the plants behind the fence were lifted up on tall boxes, while shorter boxes were used under the plants in front of the fence.

Be sure to put down clear plastic to protect the carpet, tucking in the edges of the plastic so it won't be seen. Soften the edges of the arch and gazebo with yards and yards of white net. It is not expensive and is very wide, so it covers well. Tie beautiful big bows and billow them out to complete the look. Net looks best when it is used quite extravagantly like this, so let yourself go!

The great thing about decorating with live plants is that you have them to dress up your garden after the wedding, or you can give them to family and friends as a memento of your wedding day.

GORGEOUS BASKET

You can make this wonderful basket to hold programs for your wedding or maps to your reception. It will look beautiful anywhere you place it and, after the wedding, it will be lovely in your new home.

MATERIALS

large basket
4 dried white roses
pink and purple statice
purple and white baby's breath
small amounts of larkspur, fern, hydrangea and moss
1 yard of 1¹/₂" wide wired ribbon
glue gun
narrow satin ribbon

INSTRUCTIONS

1 Glue moss all the way around the edge of the basket. Glue stems of statice into the moss on each side of the handle. Tuck in two white roses on each side. Fill in with hydrangea and larkspur. Make this area extra full as shown in the photograph.

2 Glue small sprigs of flowers into the moss all around the edge of the basket. Add sprigs of baby's breath and fern for a soft, wispy effect.

3 Tie a bow from wired ribbon, following the instructions on pages 70-71. Glue the bow to the handle, in among the flowers. Shape the bow into a pleasing shape.

4 Roll your programs into scrolls. Tie them with tiny satin bows in a color to match your flowers and the romantic look is complete.

FOR YOUR ATTENDANTS

RING BEARER'S PILLOW

A tiny ring bearer and flower girl are always so adorable. Make this elegant pillow and basket for them to carry down the aisle. You can buy a plain satin pillow and tiny basket, then add your own special touch.

MATERIALS

satin pillow with lace ruffle
5 yards wired ribbon
1 yard satin ribbon
1 pearl spray
glue gun

INSTRUCTIONS

1 Glue ribbon around the edge of the satin pillow where the lace edge begins. Shape the ribbon in a graceful up-and-down manner as shown in the photograph and glue to hold this shape.

2 Make a basic bow from the wired ribbon with three loops about 2" long on each side, following the instructions on pages 70-71. Leave the ribbon tail 10" long. Tie a 20" length of ribbon to the bow. Cut the ribbon ends on the diagonal and leave them long.

3 Fold the one yard of satin ribbon in half and glue it to the center of the pillow. Use this ribbon to tie the rings to the pillow. Glue the bow on top of this ribbon in the center of the pillow.

4 Make a shirred ribbon rose, following the instructions on pages 68-69. Glue this rose to the center of the bow. Tuck in a pearl spray and glue to hold it in place.

FLOWER GIRL'S BASKET

MATERIALS

tiny basket
white enamel spray paint
6 yards wired ribbon
pearl spray
glue gun

INSTRUCTIONS

1 Spray the basket with the white enamel paint.

2 Take one end of the ribbon and knot it to one end of the handle. Wrap the ribbon tightly around the handle. Knot the ribbon to the other end of the handle, leaving a tail about 8" long. Use a dab of glue to hold the knots in place.

3 Glue ribbon around the edge of the basket in a graceful up-and-down manner as shown in the photograph.

4 Make a basic bow with five loops about 3" long on each side, following the instructions on pages 70-71. Leave the ribbon tail 10" long. Tie 20" of ribbon to the bow. Glue the bow over one knot on the handle, then glue a 10" length of ribbon under the bow so there are five ribbon streamers. Cut the ribbon ends on the diagonal.

5 Make a shirred ribbon rose following the instructions on pages 68-69. Glue this rose to the center of the bow. Glue in a pearl spray for the finishing touch.

Special Touches

Crown of Flowers

Make these beautiful accessories to give your wedding that special touch. Plain gloves are transformed with a few ribbon roses and pearls. Silk flowers, pearls and ribbon make a beautiful crown. The wonderful garter has a special story. It was made of lace from Sylvia Eckhardt's wedding gown and given to her new daughter-in-law, Veronica, to wear on her wedding day.

MATERIALS

2 lengths of wire, each 20" long
white florists' tape
1 yard white florists' ribbon
10 stems of lily-of-the-valley
15 light-colored silk flowers
20 darker colored tiny silk flowers
8 pearl stamens
small amounts of dried ferns and baby's breath (both light- and dark-colored)
6 yards of ⅛" wide satin ribbon
glue gun

INSTRUCTIONS

1 Twist the two lengths of wire together and wrap them with white florists' tape. Wrap again, this time with white florists' ribbon. Bend each end of the wire over ½", forming a loop to attach the ribbon. This method allows you to adjust the crown to fit any size.

2 Twist the ten stems of lily-of-the-valley evenly around the ribbon-covered wire and glue them in place. Glue on the light and dark flower heads, arranging them in a pleasing fashion. Tuck in the pearls, fern and baby's breath, and glue to hold them in place. Be sure to include some darker colored flowers to add depth and dimension.

3 Cut long ribbon streamers from the six yards of ribbon and tie them through the wire loops at each end of the crown. Tie these streamers in a bow.

Lovely Gloves

MATERIALS

pair plain gloves
10 tiny ribbon roses with leaves
4 pearl stamens
4 tiny pearl leaves (optional)
glue gun

INSTRUCTIONS

1 Sew or glue three tiny ribbon roses with leaves, evenly spaced around the cuff of each glove.

2 Cut the stems very short on the pearl stamens. Glue two stamens of pearls to each glove under the leaves of the left- and right-hand flower.

3 Place a ribbon rose at an angle on each side of the center rose. Pull the pearls out around the rose. Glue the rose in place. Tuck in the tiny pearl leaves and you have a beautiful pair of custom gloves.

GARTER

Making a garter from the lace of your mother's wedding gown is such a sentimental touch. You can embellish it with pearls and sequins and add a blue bow to make it perfect! You will find an easy-to-follow pattern in the fabric stores.

The Wedding Reception

Your wedding reception should be fun; a time to relax and enjoy your guests. This chapter presents those easy-to-do final touches that will make your reception unforgettable. There are ideas for a formal candlelight reception and for a less formal garden reception. You will love the fabulous cake top and wedding flag. Provide your guests with birdseed (much better for the environment than rice) or dried rose petals to toss, and hundreds of balloons to release as you dash off to your honeymoon.

JUDI

ROMANTIC CANDLELIGHT

CENTERPIECE

If you have planned an elegant candlelight wedding ceremony, you will want to carry that romantic feeling through into your reception. This gorgeous setting captures that mood with just a small amount of fabric, ribbon, net and a candle for the centerpiece.

MATERIALS

1 yard of 45" wide gold lamé
1 yard of 72" wide white net (this is enough fabric for 4 centerpieces)
1 tall hurricane glass, candle and candle holder for each table
1 1/2 yards of 1/2" wide gold ribbon for each table
6" wired ribbon

INSTRUCTIONS

1 Cut each yard of gold lamé and white net in half. Cut each of these pieces in half again. This will give you four pieces of gold lamé, approximately 18" x 22" each and four pieces of white net approximately 18" x 36" each.

2 Place the gold lamé in the center of the table. Place the candle holder, candle and hurricane glass in the center. Arrange the lamé around the base of the hurricane glass by turning under the edges and pushing them towards the glass, making gentle folds.

3 Arrange the white net around the base of the candle, on top of the lamé. Don't pull the net tight but allow it to billow out.

4 Tie a bow around the hurricane glass with the 1 1/2 yards of ribbon, allowing the ends to cascade around the netting.

5 Make the gold napkin ring from the 6" of wired ribbon with the ends glued together.

Easy yet elegant!

TWINKLING NET

Big puffs of white net, glistening with tiny white lights are so romantic and, at the same time, so festive. This is a wonderful way to decorate doorways, around the walls at ceiling height or anywhere you want to add a special touch. Just tie up the net with white satin ribbon and puff it out to be quite full and billowy. Arrange the lights inside the net.

GLAMOROUS GOLD

NAPKIN RING

A lovely touch to your elegant formal reception is this striking gold ribbon rose napkin ring, designed by Sharon Ruth of Rolf Gille Imports, San Francisco, California. The party favor and napkin ring are easy to make and provide a wonderful memento of your wedding for your guests.

MATERIALS

For each ring

36" of 1$^1/_2$" wide gold lamé wired ribbon
1$^3/_4$" dowel or cardboard paper towel tube
clothespin
1 yard gold instant bow ribbon
9" gold-edged tulle circle
white florists' tape

INSTRUCTIONS

1 Cut a 10" length of gold wired ribbon and wrap it around the dowel or paper towel tube. Twist the ribbon and fasten the ends with a clothespin.

2 Tie a square knot with one end of the instant bow ribbon, between the clothespin and the dowel. Remove the clothespin.

3 Place the tulle circle on a flat surface and gather it, accordion-style, across the center. Tie it to the gold wired ribbon with the instant bow ribbon.

4 Make a shirred ribbon rose from the remaining 26" length of gold wired ribbon, following the instructions on pages 68-69. Tie the wires to hold the rose together. Trim these wire ends to 2" and wrap them with white florists' tape.

5 Tie the wire stem of the ribbon rose to the napkin ring with the instant bow ribbon. Push the ribbon along the gathering cord on the instant bow ribbon to create a dazzling bow. Trim the cord ends and cut the gold wired ribbon ends into a V shape. Place a pretty napkin through the loop.

GOLD PARTY FAVOR

MATERIALS

For each favor

9" gold-patterned tulle circle
9" gold-edged tulle circle
tiny plastic dish for candy or nuts
sugar-coated candy or nuts
clothespin
3 tiny gold ribbon roses
12" narrow gold ribbon

INSTRUCTIONS

1 Place the gold-patterned tulle circle on a flat surface and put the gold-edged tulle circle on top.

2 Place the plastic dish off-center, about 3" from the front edge of the tulle. Fill the dish with candy or nuts. Gather the tulle over the candy and fasten it with the clothespin. Twist the wire stems of the three ribbon roses together and wrap them around the tulle, between the candy and the clothespin.

3 Tie the 12" of narrow ribbon around the tulle, over the wire, between the candy and the clothespin. Remove the clothespin and tie the ribbon in a bow.

Goblets and Cake Knife

Some beautiful wired ribbon, a touch of pearls and a length of gold ribbon are all you need to achieve this beautiful effect on your goblets and cake knife. So very easy to do, yet so very elegant!

MATERIALS

For each bow
24" of 2" wide wired ribbon
2 pearl stamens
20" of ¹/2" wide gold ribbon
goblets
cake knife

INSTRUCTIONS

1 Fold the 2" wide wired ribbon in half to find the center point. Make a loop on either side, pinching between your thumb and index finger at the center point. Adjust the size of the loops to fit the proportions of your goblets, leaving the ribbon tails long.

2 Wrap the wires from the two pearl stamens around this center point to hold the bow together. Tie with the 20" length of gold ribbon.

3 Use the ribbon tails of the gold ribbon to tie the bows to the stem of the goblets and to the handle of the cake knife. Cut the ribbon ends in a V shape and arrange them attractively. The wired ribbon will hold any shape you like.

"The highest love of all finds its fulfilment not in what it keeps, but in what it gives."

Fr. Andrew SDC

THE RECEPTION SETTING

The reception room for our daughter's wedding was quite large and difficult to decorate. We were able to achieve a romantic feeling in the room with lighting. Branches cut from scrub oak trees were placed in large buckets of sand and grouped in clusters around the room. Some of the trees were so tall that the tops had to be wired to the walls. The buckets were draped with green fabric to conceal them from view. Finally the trees were loaded with tiny white lights, the fixed not the twinkling kind. White spotlights on the floor behind the trees shone up throughout the branches, creating an interesting pattern on the high ceiling and contributing to the fairytale atmosphere. All the overhead lights were dimmed way down and the romantic mood was set.

SPECTACULAR CAKE TOP

The cake top opposite is made from a pearl headband and beautiful organza flowers from a hair comb. The base is plastic, but it is covered by the wonderful flowers.

MATERIALS

22" pearl headband on heavy wire
2 round, plastic bases: one approximately 3^1/$_2$" across and the other approximately 2^1/$_2$" across, each about 2" high (or 1 base 4" high)
2 sprays of large organza flowers
10 silk flowers about 1" across
2 packages of pearl sprays
glue gun

INSTRUCTIONS

1 Find the center point of the pearl headband and pinch it in to form the center top of the heart. Hold this point in your hand and bend the rest of the wire to form the heart shape.

2 Glue the smaller base to the top of the larger one. Glue the bottom of the heart to the top of the base. Most of the bases have holes so you can cut the wire on the bottom of the heart and push it through the holes. Glue to secure.

3 Cut the floral spray apart and glue one large flower in the center of the base. Glue another large flower slightly lower on each side of the center flower. Glue some of the petals and leaves up the sides of the heart and around the base.

4 Cut the stems off the silk flowers and glue the flower heads all around the plastic base to cover it completely. Don't forget to fill in on the back as well. Glue in the pearl sprays and you have an elegant cake top that is unique.

Left: A beautiful wedding cake is the culmination of your wedding reception. This cake is adorned with fresh flowers and ribbons.

Opposite: Make this spectacular cake top out of a pearl headband and organza flowers from the craft store.

GARDEN RECEPTION CENTERPIECE

Carry a fresh outdoors feeling into your reception with a lovely garden flower centerpiece. You can use whatever flowers you like for this centerpiece as long as you follow the same general shape and size.

MATERIALS

For each arrangement

oasis
8" white basket with plastic container
florists' tape
2 yards of 3" wide ribbon (with patterns on both sides)
5 stems of larkspur (white, tall and slender)
7 rosebuds
9 mini carnations
5 stems of leptosporum (pink, tall and slender)
2 stems of sweet william (large cluster, dark color)
4 stems of tiny lavender asters
5 stems of tree fern
a few wispy twigs
moss
tiny bird

INSTRUCTIONS

1 Soak the oasis in water. Cut it to stand 3/4" higher than the container. Secure with florists' tape criss-crossed across the top.

2 Establish the height and line of your design by placing the tall larkspur into the oasis, slightly to the left of center. Place some shorter stems of larkspur at the base, pointing out and down on the right side. Place three roses at various heights along the line to highlight the shape.

3 Make a bow with three loops about 4" long on each side, following the basic bow instructions on pages 70-71. Leave the tail on the bow 10" long. Tie the bow with a 15" length of ribbon. Glue this bow to the left side of the basket. Pull the tie ends down and glue the right-hand end to the basket as shown. Pull the 10" bow tail up and out of the way while you complete the arrangement.

4 Fill in with the other flowers. The back of your arrangement should look like the front. Place the twigs last of all. Glue a nest of moss on the lower right side and tuck in the tiny bird.

5 Arrange the 10" ribbon tail up through the flowers and glue it in several places. If your basket does not have a handle, just pull the ribbon up through the flowers. Cut all the ribbon ends on the diagonal.

SAY IT WITH FLOWERS

Give flowers to your parents, grandparents, candlelighters, guest book attendant, reception servers, special relatives and the pastor (unless he wears a robe). Pin the corsage and the boutonnière on the left side with the stem down. For a tender touch, take a single rose to each mother as you leave the church.

Wedding Flag

Adorned with a floral heart and ribbon streamers, this beautiful flag is a festive way to announce to your guests the location of the reception. It will be extra special if you make it from fabric left over from your bridesmaids' dresses. Of course, you can make it from any fabric you choose as long as it has a sheen and some body. The big bonus is that there is nothing to sew!

MATERIALS

1 yard plain fabric
small amount of iron-on fusible webbing
pencil
craft glue
4 yards of each color ribbon (we used 3 colors of $^1/8$" wide and 2 colors of $^1/4$" wide satin ribbon)
$^1/4$ yard of floral print fabric (small flowers with green leaves or ivy work best)
36" of $^1/2$" dowel
3 thumb tacks

INSTRUCTIONS

1 Fold the plain fabric in half with the right sides out. Turn under a small hem all around on the raw edges. Iron on the fusible webbing to hold it together. The finished measurement of the flag is 19" x 33".

2 Lightly draw a large heart on the front of the flag with the pencil. Glue two colors of $^1/4$" wide ribbon around this line in a graceful up-and-down manner as shown.

3 Cut the flowers and greens out of the print fabric and arrange them around the ribbon heart shape. Experiment until you are pleased with your arrangement then glue it in place. Scatter a few extra leaves or ivy around.

4 Make a tie bow from each color of the $^1/4$" wide ribbon, following the instructions on page 71. Leave the ribbon ends long. Glue the two bows together at the center top of the heart. Glue the ribbon tails down as shown.

5 Attach your flag to the dowel with tacks, at each end and in the middle.

6 Make tie bows with each color of the $^1/8$" ribbons and any leftover $^1/4$" ribbon. Leave the ribbon tails about 8" long. Glue one bow of each

CHILDHOOD MEMORIES

A table arrayed with childhood photos of the bride and groom is a tender touch to add to the reception. Make sure you include photos of the different ages and stages in their lives before meeting each other. Include some pictures of the two of them together during their dating period and place their engagement photo in the center. Cluster the groom's baby pictures on one side and the bride's on the other. Decorate the table with flowers and romantic embellishments.

color on the top of the flag at the ends. Glue on the remaining ribbon as streamers to blow in the wind.

Above: *Welcome your guests to your reception with a pretty wedding flag.*

Right: *Add a touch of nostalgia with a collection of childhood photographs.*

Down Memory Lane

After all the excitement of your wedding day, life will begin to calm down and you will be busy settling into your new home.

This chapter tells you how to capture the special memories of the biggest day in your life in keepsakes. Dry the flowers from your bouquet to make a wreath or garland or save an aisle bow to decorate and hang in your bedroom. These are just a few of the ideas included in this chapter.

File this book away and take it out for ideas when you plan your twenty-fifth wedding anniversary celebration.

JUDI

Hearts and Roses

Lace Basket

Jan Mattos made this beautiful lace box to hold fragrant potpourri from her wedding flowers. The heart pin and ring box were embellished with a collection of pearl buttons gathered from a favorite aunt, grandmother and mother, and from the wedding dress.

MATERIALS

white wicker basket or box with lid
plastic for lining the basket
glue gun
moss
small lace pillow to fit lid
2 yards of lace trim
dried roses
potpourri
fern

INSTRUCTIONS

1 Line the basket with plastic. Glue moss all around the opening edge.

Glue the lace pillow to the inside of the lid. Glue the lace trim all around the edge of the lid and around the base on the outside of the basket.

2 Glue dried roses and fern into the moss around the edge of the basket opening.

3 Fill with fragrant potpourri. Fill the bottom half of the basket or box with crumpled tissue paper so that only a thin layer of potpourri is necessary.

Heart Pin and Ring Box

MATERIALS

small plastic heart box
small wooden heart shape for a pin
interesting buttons and beads
pearl stamens
gold braid
heart and cherub charms
white felt
pin back
white ribbon or gold cord

INSTRUCTIONS

1 Arrange the buttons in an interesting pattern on top of the heart box or wooden shape. Add dimension to your arrangement by gluing some buttons on top of others, placing the more interesting ones on top.

2 Tuck in a few pearls to cover any backing that shows around the edge. Embellish with pearl stamens, charms, beads and gold cord.

3 To complete the pin, glue white felt to the back of the wooden heart shape and then glue a pin back in the center, near the top. Glue white ribbon or gold cord around the edge to conceal the wood.

You could make a pin with special buttons for your mother and new mother-in-law as a sentimental gift!

KEEPSAKE WREATH

Have someone dry the flowers from your bridal bouquet while you are on your honeymoon. They will need to take the bouquet apart so that air can circulate around each flower, then hang the flowers upside down in a dark place for three to four weeks.

MATERIALS

dried flowers, various sizes
heart-shaped wreath form
spray paint
4 yards wired ribbon
small amount of Spanish moss
glue gun

INSTRUCTIONS

1 Spray paint the wreath form in the color of your choice. Glue a small amount of Spanish moss to the bottom of the wreath and slightly up the left side.

2 Glue some tall slender flowers to the left side of the wreath, cutting the stems at different lengths. Extend a few stems up past the top of the wreath. Fill in with the other flowers as shown. The final look of the wreath will vary according to the type of flowers you have available. You might want to purchase some preserved greens to add to the wreath.

3 Make a bow with two loops about 5" long on each side, following the instructions on pages 70-71. Cut the ribbon tail 15" long. Tie a 20" length of ribbon to the bow. Glue the bow to the center of the wreath. Cut a length of ribbon 15" long and glue it under the bow so you have four ribbon streamers. Cascade these streamers through the arrangement of flowers, with the longer ribbons to the outside. Trim all the ribbon ends on the diagonal.

MEMENTOS

WEDDING INVITATION FRAME

Preserve your wedding invitation in a heart-shaped frame with a touch of satin, lace and flowers.

The wonderful lace pillow was made by Frances Lawler to hold all the bows and ribbons from your shower gifts. Every time you admire the pillow, it will help you to remember all those who love you and wished you well.

MATERIALS

small pieces of satin and lace fabrics
heart-shaped frame
1 yard wired ribbon
silk flowers and fern
glue gun

INSTRUCTIONS

1 Cut the satin and lace fabrics to fit the inside of the frame. Center your invitation on the fabric and secure it in the frame.

2 Make a tie bow following the directions on pages 70-71. Glue the silk flowers and fern and the bow to the upper left side of the frame.

LACE PILLOW

To make the pretty lace pillow, find a pattern and lace that you like in the fabric store. Make the pillow, leaving an opening in the back. Fill the pillowcase with all your bows and ribbons. Sew on a length of satin ribbon to each side of the opening and tie them in a bow to close the pillowcase.

TIED WITH FLOWERS

ACCORDION FILE

Every bride needs a file to organize the many notes and receipts accumulated for the wedding. Decorate a plain accordion file with some beautiful fabric and you can use it after the wedding for your monthly bills or recipes.

MATERIALS

small amount of batting
craft glue
paperboard accordion file
$1/2$ yard of fabric
small amount of fusible webbing
1 yard of 1" wide satin ribbon

INSTRUCTIONS

1 Glue the batting to the front and back of the file up to $3/4$" from the edges. This gap will allow you to glue the fabric directly to the file later.

2 Place the fabric on the file, centering the design on the front.

Measure from edge to edge over the batting, then add a 1" seam allowance all the way around. Trim the fabric to this measurement.

3 Turn in and press the 1" seam allowance. Secure it with fusible webbing. Glue along the $3/4$" gap at the edge of the file. Place the fabric on the glue, pressing it down firmly to hold. It is best to glue one section at a time.

4 Cut the ribbon in half and glue one end under the top flap and another under the bottom of the file so you can tie a bow to close it.

AISLE BOW

MATERIALS

4 yards of 3" wide florists' ribbon
dried flowers
small bird
1 yard of ¹/8" wide satin ribbon

INSTRUCTIONS

1 Make a florists' bow from wired ribbon with five loops about 5" long on each side, following the instructions on page 71. Cut the tail even with the loops. Tie a 25" length of ribbon to the bow.

2 Glue the dried flowers to the center of the bow and tuck in a small bird.

3 Glue narrow ribbon streamers through the flowers. Cut a 22" length of narrow ribbon and glue each end into the bow to form the hanger. Hang it from a door handle or bed post to remember your special day!

Save a bow used to decorate the aisle at your wedding. Add a few flowers, dainty ribbon and a bird for another wonderful keepsake.

TWIG FLOWER GARLAND

Create a beautiful memento of your wedding with flowers from your ceremony and reception decor. Dry them upside down in a dark place, allowing the air to circulate freely around each flower.

This striking garland is easy to make and will be a wonderful accent in your new home.

MATERIALS

small amounts of fern, twigs and moss
florists' wire
2 yards of 3" wide wired ribbon
long slender flowers such as larkspur or
    statice (some dark- and some light-
    colored)
10 dried roses
glue gun

INSTRUCTIONS

1 Arrange the twigs in two bundles that are exactly the same size. Wrap wire around each bundle. Wire the stem ends together, overlapping them for approximately 2" and glue to secure.

2 To hide the wire, glue moss all around where the two bundles are joined.

3 Make a tie bow with the loops about 6" long, following the instructions on pages 70-71. Leave the ribbon tails long and the same length on each side. Wire and glue the bow to the center of the twig bundle.

4 Glue the long slender flowers into the moss and twigs on both sides of the bow. Be sure to have dark- and light-colored flowers to add depth and dimension to your arrangement. Glue in the roses close to the bow.

5 Arrange the ribbon ends through the garland and glue them in place. Glue in the fern and extra twigs for fullness.

I love you, not only for what you are, but for what I am when I am with you.

I love you, not only for what you have made of yourself but for what you are making of me.

I love you for the part of me that you bring out; I love you for putting your hand into my heaped-up heart and passing over all the foolish, weak things that you can't help dimly seeing there, and for drawing out into the light all the beautiful belongings that no one else had looked quite far enough to find.

I love you because you are helping me to make of the lumber of my life not a tavern but a temple; Out of the works of my every day not a reproach but a song.....

Author unknown

Sweet Remembrance

Video Box Cover

What a fabulous way to store your wedding video! The box is covered in moiré taffeta with a ribbon rose tucked into the bow. You can add a ribbon rose , following the directions on pages 68-69.

Impress your new husband with this delicious dessert, while you enjoy your wedding video.

MATERIALS

small amount of batting
craft glue
^{1}/3 yard fabric
2 yards of ^{3}/4" wide ribbon
12" of 1" wide wired ribbon for a rose (optional)
5" of 1" wide green wired ribbon for a leaf (optional)
1 pearl stamen

INSTRUCTIONS

1 Glue the batting around the front and back of the video box. Do not glue inside the box where the video slides in or on the ends of the box.

2 Measure the fabric to fit around the box over the batting, allowing for ^{1}/2" overlap on all sides.

3 Place the fabric on the box, over the batting, and fold the corners as you would on a gift package. Glue the edges to hold the fabric in place. Turn the fabric to the inside of the front of the box and glue it flat so the video can slide in.

4 Glue ribbon all around the edge of the box to cover the edge. Fold a 24" length of ribbon in half and glue it to the open edge of the box to use as a tie and to hold the video in place. Make a bow with three loops on each side about 2^1/2" long, following the instructions on pages 70-71.

5 Tie a 7" length of ribbon to the bow. Glue the bow over the ribbon tie on the front of the box.

Old-Fashioned Apple Crisp

SERVES 6

4 cups tart apples, sliced and pared
^{1}/3 cup orange juice
1 cup sugar
^{3}/4 cup flour
^{1}/2 teaspoon cinnamon
^{1}/4 teaspoon nutmeg
pinch of salt
^{1}/2 cup butter or margarine

METHOD

1 Preheat the oven to 375°F. Place the apples in a buttered 9" pie plate, molding them up in the center and keeping those on the edge even with the sides of the plate. Sprinkle with orange juice.

2 For the topping, combine sugar, flour, spices and salt. Cut in the butter, or margarine, with a fork or pastry blender until mixture is crumbly. Spread over the apples. All the apples should be covered with topping so they won't dry out in the oven.

3 Place the pie plate on a cookie sheet in case the apples bubble over. Bake in the oven at 375°F for 45 minutes or until the apples are very soft when pierced with a fork and the topping is crisp and lightly browned.

4 Serve warm with a scoop of vanilla ice cream or with a pitcher of light cream.

POSIES AND PICTURES

NOSEGAY

This adorable bundle of dried flowers is another wonderful keepsake made from your bridal bouquet. Display it anywhere you want to add a dainty touch.

MATERIALS

bouquet or floral arrangement
3 yards of 1¹/2" wide wired ribbon
florists' wire
glue gun

INSTRUCTIONS

1 Pull apart the bouquet or flower arrangement so the air can circulate freely around each flower. Dry the flowers by hanging them upside down in a dark place for about three to four weeks. For best results, this must be done while the flowers are still fresh, so have someone dry them for you while you are on your honeymoon.

2 Make a basic bow with three loops about 5" long on each side, following the instructions on pages 70-71. Cut the ribbon tails even with the loops and tie a 12" length of ribbon to the bow.

3 Make a tiny bouquet of dried flowers and tie the bow around them at the base of the flower heads. Wrap the flower stems with a piece of ribbon and glue to hold the ends in place. Fluff out the bow around the flowers. Pull the ribbon tie ends out and cut them on the diagonal.

FLORAL PICTURE FRAME

MATERIALS

plastic frame with stand
1 yard narrow ribbon
*5 tiny silk roses and 5 violets (or similar-
    sized flowers)*
sprigs of pepper grass and fern
glue gun

INSTRUCTIONS

1 We used a 5" x 7" frame for a
4" x 6" photograph. If your frame is
larger, you will need more ribbon and
flowers. Center the photograph in the
frame and tape it in place.

2 Make a tie bow from narrow
ribbon, following the instructions
on pages 70-71, leaving the ribbon tails
long. Glue the bow on the top left-
hand corner and twist the ribbon ends
as shown in the photograph, gluing as
you go.

3 Glue two violets under the bow
together with two tiny silk roses.
Glue three violets and three tiny silk
roses to the bottom right-hand corner.
Tuck in a few sprigs of pepper grass, or
other filler flowers, and fern. Glue to
hold in place.

*Your engagement
photograph will look
striking in this floral
frame. Choose colors
to match the decor of
your new home and
be prepared for the
compliments from
your friends.*

HOW TO MAKE A ROSE

SHIRRED RIBBON ROSE

Illustration 1: Pull the wire from one edge of a 12" length of ribbon. Push the ribbon towards the center from both ends until it is about 8" long. Place the stamen over one folded end of the ribbon as shown.

Illustration 2: Begin to wrap the ribbon around the stamen, creating a tight center.

Illustration 3: Wrap the ribbon more loosely for the outer petals of the rose.

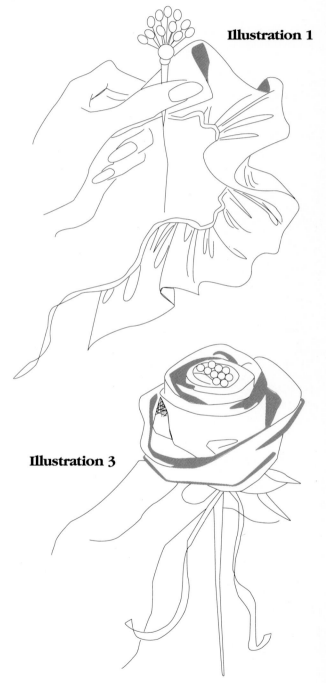

Illustration 1

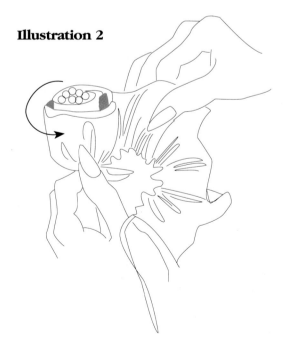

Illustration 2

Illustration 3

FOLDED RIBBON ROSE

Illustration 1: Fold down one end of a 15" length of wired ribbon. Place the stamen as shown.

Illustration 2: Place your left thumb close to the stamen as shown.

Illustration 3: Rotate the ribbon-wrapped stamen counter-clockwise, forming a diagonal fold.

Illustration 4: Continue to rotate the stamen with your fingers in the position shown until 1" of ribbon remains. Secure this end to the stem with wire.

Illustration 5: The completed rose.

Illustration 1

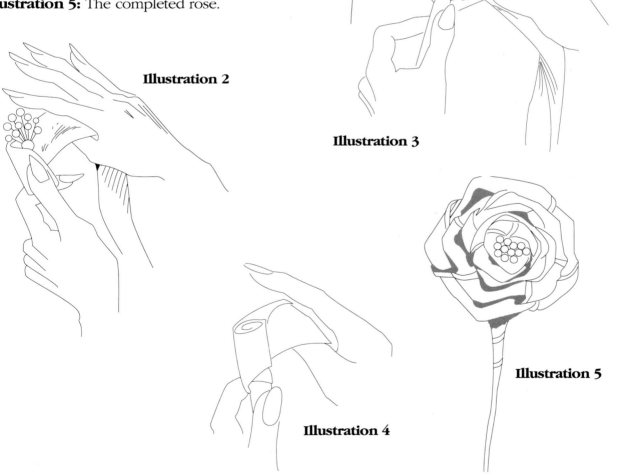

Illustration 2

Illustration 3

Illustration 4

Illustration 5

HOW TO TIE A BOW

BASIC BOW

This bow can be tricky if it is your first attempt. The secret is practice. My first bow was a disaster but I kept trying until I finally perfected it. You can do it too – just follow these simple instructions.

INSTRUCTIONS

1 Hold the ribbon right side up between your thumb and index finger. Pinch the ribbon approximately 2" from the end and then form a loop as large as you need, rolling the ribbon up and away from you. Place the long end of the ribbon between your thumb and index finger to form the bow's center. (See Illustration 1.)

Illustration 1

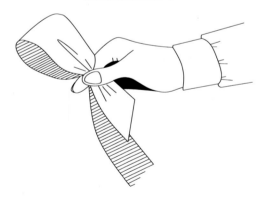

2 Before forming the bottom loop, make a half twist to the left so that the ribbon will be right side out, then roll the ribbon down and away from you. Pinch the ribbon together at the bow's center. (See Illustration 2.)

Illustration 2

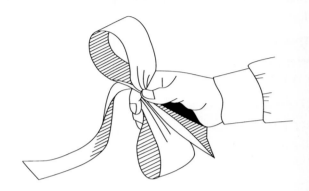

3 Continue forming loops until you have enough, keeping the loops the same size. Remember **ALWAYS** to pinch the ribbon at the center and **ALWAYS** to twist to the left before forming each loop.

4 To keep the bow from slipping, lift your index finger as you twist, momentarily using your middle finger and thumb to secure the loops until the twist is completed.

5 Once the loops are completed, cut the end of the ribbon, leaving a tail as long as required (this length will vary on each design). Now you are ready to wire.

6 To secure the bow, tie a piece of wire around the bow's center and twist the ends together tightly underneath the bow. Now arrange the loops to form a perfect bow.

7 Cut a length of ribbon (the exact length will vary for each design) to create the "tie" for the bow. Wrap the tie around the bow's center to conceal the wire. Knot the ribbon in the back.

8 Cut all the ribbon ends on the diagonal or in a V shape.

FLORISTS' BOW

INSTRUCTIONS

1 This bow is made in exactly the same way as the basic bow, except that you begin by pinching the ribbon between your thumb and index finger 4" from the end.

2 Proceed, following the instructions for the basic bow until all the loops are formed. Before you secure the bow with wire, twist the 4" end on top of the bow forming a loop and making sure it is right side out. Place the wire through the small center loop, then wire as for the basic bow. (See Illustration 1.)

Illustration 1

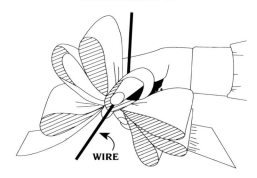

WIRE

3 Arrange the loops to form a perfect bow. Cut a length of ribbon for the "tie" for the bow. Place this ribbon through the small center loop and knot it in the back.

TIE BOW

This bow is the one used on the back of little girls' dresses, around your neck, on shoelaces and on packages. Follow these simple instructions and you will tie a perfect bow every time.

1 Starting with both ends even, cross the right ribbon underneath the left. (This is very important to keep the bow straight.) Make a half-knot as shown in Illustration 1.

Illustration 1

2 With your left hand make a loop between the thumb and index finger, keeping the wrong sides of the ribbon together. Cross over the top of the loop with the other ribbon right side up. Now, finish the second loop by pulling it up through the center space you've just created. Pull it tight.

3 To prevent the wrong side facing out on the second loop, twist the ribbon a half-turn just before taking it up through the center space. (See Illustration 2.) If the right-hand tail is wrong side out, twist the left loop and the right tail simultaneously towards you in a rolling motion.

Illustration 2

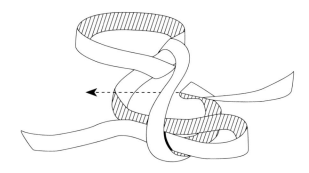

Managing Editor
Judy Poulos

Editorial Coordinator
Margaret Kelly

Layout
Tara Barrett

Production
Sheridan Carter
Christie & Eckermann

Illustrations
Tara Barrett

Photography
Todd Tsukushi

Cover Design
Christie & Eckermann

ISBN 0 937769 88 6

*A special thank you to photographer Todd Tsukushi,
Santa Cruz Photographics; Marsha Ifland, detail coordinator; Tony and
Suzy Holbrook; Jimbo, and Donna DesJarlais of The Country Court Tea Room,
911 Capitola Avenue, Capitola, California, 95010. Contributed
photography by Carvello and Carvello.*